# The Little Book of Scissor Skills

## Developing hands and fingers

by Sharon Drew

Illustrations by Martha Hardy

LITTL⌐ IDEAS

This 2nd edition published 2013 by Featherstone Education,
an imprint of Bloomsbury Publishing Plc
50 Bedford Square, London, WC1B 3DP
www.bloomsbury.com

ISBN 978-1-4729-0871-1
First published in the UK by Featherstone Education, 2008

Text © Sharon Drew, 2008
Illustrations © Martha Hardy, 2008
Series Editor, Sally Featherstone
Cover photographs © Shutterstock

Printed and bound in India by Replika Pvt. Ltd

1 3 5 7 9 10 8 6 4 2

This book is produced using paper that is made from wood grown in managed,
sustainable forests. It is natural, renewable and recyclable. The logging and
manufacturing processes conform to the environmental regulations of the country
of origin.


**To see our full range of titles visit**
**www.bloomsbury.com**

# Contents

# Introduction

This book is one of the titles in a series of Little Books, which explore aspects of practice within the Early Years Foundation Stage in England. The books are also suitable for practitioners working with the early years curriculum in Wales, Northern Ireland and Scotland, and in any early years setting catering for young children.

Across the series you will find titles appropriate to each aspect of the curriculum for children from two to five years, giving practitioners a wealth of ideas for engaging activities, interesting resources and stimulating environments to enrich their work across the early years curriculum.

Each title also has information linking the activity pages to the statutory early years curriculum for England. This title has been updated to include the revised Early Learning Goals published by the Department for Education in March 2012. The full set of 19 goals is included in the introduction to each book, and the activity pages will refer you to the relevant statements to which each activity contributes.

For the purposes of observation and assessment of the children's work in each activity, we recommend that practitioners should use each of the 'revised statements' as a whole, resisting any impulse to separate the elements of each one into short phrases.

**The key goals for this title are highlighted in purple, although other goals may be included on some pages.**

## PRIME AREAS

### Communication and language

**(1) Listening and attention:** children listen attentively in a range of situations. They listen to stories, accurately anticipating key events and respond to what they hear with relevant comments, questions or actions. They give their attention to what others say and respond appropriately, while engaged in another activity.

**(2) Understanding:** children follow instructions involving several ideas or actions. They answer 'how' and 'why' questions about their experiences and in response to stories or events.

**(3) Speaking:** children express themselves effectively, showing awareness of listeners' needs. They use past, present and future forms accurately when talking about events that have happened or are to happen in the future. They develop their own narratives and explanations by connecting ideas or events.

## Physical development

**(1) Moving and handling:** children show good control and co-ordination in large and small movements. They move confidently in a range of ways, safely negotiating space. They handle equipment and tools effectively, including pencils for writing.

**(2) Health and self-care:** children know the importance for good health of physical exercise, and a healthy diet, and talk about ways to keep healthy and safe. They manage their own basic hygiene and personal needs successfully, including dressing and going to the toilet independently.

## Personal, social and emotional development

**(1) Self-confidence and self-awareness:** children are confident to try new activities, and say why they like some activities more than others. They are confident to speak in a familiar group, will talk about their ideas, and will choose the resources they need for their chosen activities. They say when they do or don't need help.

**(2) Managing feelings and behaviour:** children talk about how they and others show feelings, talk about their own and others' behaviour, and its consequences, and know that some behaviour is unacceptable. They work as part of a group or class, and understand and follow the rules. They adjust their behaviour to different situations, and take changes of routine in their stride.

**(3) Making relationships:** children play co-operatively, taking turns with others. They take account of one another's ideas about how to organise their activity. They show sensitivity to others' needs and feelings, and form positive relationships with adults and other children.

# SPECIFIC AREAS

## Literacy

**(1) Reading:** children read and understand simple sentences. They use phonic knowledge to decode regular words and read them aloud accurately. They also read some common irregular words. They demonstrate understanding when talking with others about what they have read.

**(2) Writing:** children use their phonic knowledge to write words in ways which match their spoken sounds. They also write some irregular common words. They write simple sentences which can be read by themselves and others. Some words are spelt correctly and others are phonetically plausible.

## Mathematics

**①  Numbers:** children count reliably with numbers from 1 to 20, place them in order and say which number is one more or one less than a given number. Using quantities and objects, they add and subtract two single-digit numbers and count on or back to find the answer. They solve problems, including doubling, halving and sharing.

**②  Shape, space and measures:** children use everyday language to talk about size, weight, capacity, position, distance, time and money to compare quantities and objects and to solve problems. They recognise, create and describe patterns. They explore characteristics of everyday objects and shapes and use mathematical language to describe them.

## Understanding the world

**①  People and communities:** children talk about past and present events in their own lives and in the lives of family members. They know that other children don't always enjoy the same things, and are sensitive to this. They know about similarities and differences between themselves and others, and among families, communities and traditions.

**②  The world:** children know about similarities and differences in relation to places, objects, materials and living things. They talk about the features of their own immediate environment and how environments might vary from one another. They make observations of animals and plants and explain why some things occur, and talk about changes.

**③  Technology:** children recognise that a range of technology is used in places such as homes and schools. They select and use technology for particular purposes.

## Expressive arts and design

**①  Exploring and using media and materials:** children sing songs, make music and dance, and experiment with ways of changing them. They safely use and explore a variety of materials, tools and techniques, experimenting with colour, design, texture, form and function.

**②  Being imaginative:** children use what they have learnt about media and materials in original ways, thinking about uses and purposes. They represent their own ideas, thoughts and feelings through design and technology, art, music, dance, role-play and stories.

# How to use this book

'The Little Book of Scissor Skills' is intended for everyone who works with young children in nurseries, playgroups and of course at home. The book contains a variety of fun, easy to do activities which suit different ages, stages of development and levels of skill with scissors. All you need is some scissors, glue, simple art and craft materials, and space to make a mess! Each activity suggests what you will need and what you have to do. There are also lots of ideas about how you can extend the activities.

Cutting and sticking activities are great for developing children's fine motor skills (those skills that involve the small muscle movements of their hands and fingers in co-ordination with their eyes).

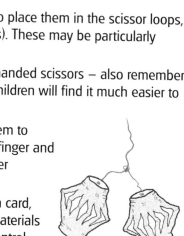

## Getting Started

Before using scissors in play and learning, we need to think about the children's overall development, and whether they are ready to hold and use tools such as scissors.

Some children are not ready to use scissors, so you need to offer other activities which can be practiced alongside to help scaffold and develop the skills they need. Here are a few tips to help:

▶ observe and think about the level the child is at before presenting a cutting task or activity;

▶ if the child is unable to isolate their fingers to place them in the scissor loops, try using long looped scissors (see resources). These may be particularly useful for children with physical disabilities;

▶ if the child is left-handed, buy and use left-handed scissors – also remember that when cutting out shapes, left-handed children will find it much easier to work in a clockwise direction;

▶ when teaching children to cut, encourage them to hold the scissors correctly, with their middle finger and thumb in the finger loops and the index finger supporting the scissor blades;

▶ start with small pieces of firmer paper or thin card, as it is easier to cut, and progress to those materials that are less resistant and more difficult to control when cutting, such as fabric or tissue paper.

## Offer activities and resources that support scissor skills

Provide opportunities through role play for the children to play with tongs or tweezers, to develop the concept of opening and closing the scissors. Such activities might include a doctor's surgery, a vets, or beauty parlour.

▶ Provide tweezers and tongs in the outside area for picking up small objects.

▶ Introduce activities where children need to pick up balls, bean bags or other small objects in games and other free play.

▶ Provide opportunities in water play, mark making, outdoor play and other creative activities to use turkey basters, water bottles, spray bottles, squirt toys, droppers, etc. This helps to develop the opening and closing action in their hands, ready for using scissors, as well as helping to strengthen the hand muscles.

▶ In creative activities, make confetti using single hole-punches or hole-punches that make different shapes (stars, hearts, etc.). This works on the open/close concept, and builds hand strength.

▶ Use clickers and castanets in music, drop, pick up and hold scarves and ribbons in dance.

▶ Use torn paper as a resource in collage and pictures. Tearing paper helps develop hand strength as well as practising how to use two hands together, which is a necessary skill for using scissors.

▶ In the home corner and outdoor play activities, provide opportunities for the children to use clothes-pegs to hang pictures, dolls clothes or number cards on a 'washing line', or to fix drapes and fabrics for clothes and shelters. Clothes pegs work on the concept of squeezing and releasing.

▶ Playing with dough using garlic presses to make 'spaghetti' or 'hair' also helps strengthen children's hands for scissor use.

## General progression for cutting shapes

There appear to be some very separate stages in the development of cutting, and practitioners should give young children plenty of practice at each stage before moving on, to avoid disappointment and frustration.

▶ Holding the scissors is the first major task, and this can sometimes be supported by offering a 'hand-over-hand' grip, with the adult's hand over the child's. Proper grip should always be demonstrated, encouraged and praised.

▶ Opening and closing the scissors in a controlled action and making random snips on the paper. At this stage, children just need paper to snip, and simple strips or shapes of any fairly strong paper will do – junk mail cut in strips about 1″ (1.5cm) wide is ideal. Help the child to practice snipping these strips, or the edges of larger shapes.

▶ Once a child has achieved some control over scissors, they will be able to try cutting along a line. Start by drawing some broad straight lines with a black felt pen across strips and shapes of paper, and helping the child to cut along the lines. Simpler is better for confidence building.

▶ As the children become more confident, offer them the challenge of wavy lines and spirals.

▶ Cutting along a line that involves one change of direction, then two, then more. As confidence grows, children will be able to navigate lines with turns and corners. However, this does need control of both hands, so they can hold the paper and the scissors and manipulate each separately. Don't under-estimate the difficulty of this, and continue to offer help and praise as they attempt this stage.

▶ Turning more corners and following more complex shapes needs much more control, and should only be offered to children who have had plenty of experience of simple cutting. You could start with simplified, adult-drawn shapes such as vehicles, chunky figures and shapes of all sorts. Colouring books often have ideal pictures for this stage, with broad outlines and simple shapes.

▶ Cutting out their own drawings. This is often the stage where confidence ebbs and children become frustrated by the fiddly lines they draw in their own pictures, resulting in cutting off important parts, such as legs and arms! Try drawing a circle or square round the whole picture, or a cutting line that follows the general shape of the picture, to make this task easier at first, and encourage children to draw bigger by giving them felt pens or thick crayons.

## Teach scissor safety

Put scissors down when you are not using them. Only cut things you know are allowed. Scissors are sharp – mind your fingers! Never put scissors in your mouth. Carry scissors with the blades closed, and in the palm of your hand.

## Ages and stages

The usual developmental progression of scissor control is:

▶ At around age 2: Children can hold scissors using two hands. They can often use one hand to snip, but need someone else to hold the paper. At this stage, children are involved in the action of cutting and snipping, not 'cutting out'. At this stage they also enjoy applying glue and paste with spreaders and brushes to flat surfaces such as card and thick paper, but the concept of sticking something to something else may not yet have developed. The spreading is the thing!

▶ At around 3: Many children can use one hand to hold the scissors. However, some may still find it difficult to hold and manipulate the paper at the same time, so they may need a little help. With some help and encouragement they can usually make continuous cuts across paper.

▶ By the ages of 4 or 4+: Children's hands are usually developmentally ready to operate scissors with one hand and the paper with the other.

> **Girls and boys**: many girls will be able to control scissors at a younger age than many boys, so be understanding of the frustration shown by some boys when learning how to use scissors. Give them more time and use praise to keep them motivated.

# Activities for younger children and children with additional needs

### Sandpaper snip

Invite the children to cut up pieces of light grade sand paper. This is easier for a young child to cut than paper. Children could colour the sandpaper with crayons before cutting it. Sandpaper does blunt scissors!

### Cotton material cutting

The day before you offer this activity, take cotton material of any colour or pattern. Paint glue all over it, let it dry, then use it the next day for children to cut out the patterns or make their own cuttings. The glue makes the material stiff and much easier for children to cut. To fold and cut your art, provide the children with a square of wrapping paper each. Show them how to fold the square in half several times. Help the children to make small cuts along the folded edges of the paper. Let them unfold the square to reveal the cut-out designs. For variation, try newspaper, flattened coffee filters, or doilies.

## Foil art

Provide each child with several sheets of aluminum foil. Encourage them to form and mould the foil, cutting where needed to make strips or new sections. Show the children how to make snips in the foil and how to fold the foil in different directions.

## Dough creation

Cutting dough is a great way for young children to develop cutting skills. Roll the dough into a 'log', and then encourage the children to cut it into smaller pieces. Try flattening the dough into a 'pancake' and make small cuts all around the outside of the circle.

## Finger songs for scissor skills

Using finger play games and songs also help to develop scissor skills and call attention to individual finger movements. Try these:

## Open shut them

Open, shut them, open, shut them, open, shut them.
(use index and middle finger to make scissors motion)

Give a little snip, snip, snip.
(three quick snips with fingers)

Open, shut them, open, shut them.
(repeat scissors motion)

Make another clip.
(make another scissor motion)

## Snip snip snip

I take my scissors, snip, snip, snip
and cut the paper into bits.

Some are round and some are square,
Some have patterns everywhere.

# Snip-snap!

**Focus**
**Simple cutting and snipping**

**Skills**
**Snipping**

## What you need:

▶ Paper, wool, ribbon, fabric, raffia, string, leaves, grass, and anything else 'snippable'

▶ A range of different types and sizes of scissors

# What you do:

This simple activity will help children gain basic control of scissors and practice simple cutting. You can use any materials that are easy to cut, so use your imagination and offer as wide a range as possible.

1. Look at all the materials together and talk about what they are, how they look and how they feel. Look at the different scissors and let the children choose which ones they would like to use. Be aware of children who may find it easier to use looped or left-handed versions, and make sure they have the option of using these.

2. Sit with the children and demonstrate how to make simple cuts and snips in the materials you have collected together.

3. The children should feel free to experiment with different types of scissors for different materials.

## And another idea

▶ Collect all the snippings and use them for a collage.

▶ Take some round-ended scissors out of doors or on a trip to the park, where you can collect natural materials and sit for a snipping session. Make sure you are snipping things that are already dead or don't matter!

## Look, listen and note

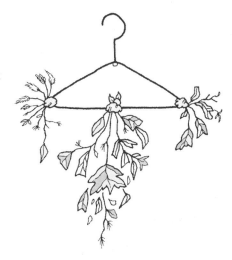

▶ Watch as the children work, and note any who are having difficulty. Listen to their conversations as they work, and encourage them to talk about the way the materials feel and whether they are easy or difficult to cut.

▶ Make a note of any children who need help, and what they are finding particularly difficult, so you can plan more activities to help them practice the skills they need.

# You are my sunshine

**Focus**
A simple pegging activity

**Skills**
Strengthening fingers and hands

## What you need:

▶ Paper plates

▶ Yellow paint

▶ Plenty of yellow clothes-pegs of different sorts and sizes

# What you do:

Working with pegs is a good preparation for cutting with scissors, as it strengthens the muscles of the hands and fingers, and the pincer grip of the finger and thumb. Collect as many different pegs as you can – different sorts, sizes and types, wooden, plastic, big and small.

1. Start with a pile of pegs and try pegging one peg onto another to make a long line. Now clip pegs all the way round pieces of card, along washing lines, or on the edges of stiff fabric. The children could clip the pegs onto their own or their friends' clothes. Use pegs to fix scarves and other fabrics for dressing up, or shelter making.

2. Make some sunshine peg patterns by painting a paper plate yellow and pegging yellow pegs all round the edge.

3. Draw a sunshine face in the mddle of the plate and hang them all up as a mobile.

## And another idea

▶ Clip pegs round the edge of a clean empty tin. Big tins work best, and make sure you smooth any sharp bits.

▶ Peg letters, numbers, shapes, pictures on washing lines. Use them to sequence stories, sing counting songs and make words.

▶ Make the longest peg chain you can, on the floor or a table, using all the pegs you can find. Have a peg chain race, and see who can make the longest chain using a sand timer to keep time.

## Look, listen and note

▶ Observe the way individual children manage pegs - the operation needs strength and dexterity.

▶ Offer all children plenty of games and simple activities that are quick, fun and develop finger and hand strength and dexterity.

# Fringes on the edges

**Focus**
**Another simple snipping activity**

**Skills**
**Snipping lines**

## What you need:

▶ Lengths of paper or card, in different colours

▶ A range of different types and sizes of scissors

▶ Glue sticks (optional)

I will need

# What you do:

This activity puts a bit of structure into snipping, by encouraging the use of both hands and snipping along an edge. You can use any paper or thin card that is easy to cut, but make sure it is firm enough to handle in the hand that doesn't hold the scissors.

1. Look at all the strips together and talk about what you are going to do. Look at the different scissors and let the children choose which ones they would like to use. Be aware of children who may find it easier to use looped or left handed versions, and make sure they have the option of using these.

2. Sit with the children and demonstrate how to make simple cuts along the edge of the strips of paper, to make fringes.

3. The children should feel free to experiment with different types of scissors as they fringe the edges.

## And another idea

▶ Use coloured paper to make fringed flowers. Fold some strips in half. Unfold them and fringe both sides, making sure you don't go too near the fold (a felt pen stop line may help some children).

▶ Re-fold the fringed strips and roll them round a lolly stick or short cane. Stick the ends down and spread the fringes out to make petals.

## Look, listen and note

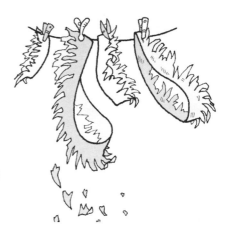

▶ Watch as the children work, and note any who are having difficulty. Listen to their conversations as they work, and encourage them to talk about the fringing and how they are managing the task.

▶ Make a note of any children who need help, and leave fringing activities in the art area for free choice times.

# Flower cups

**Focus**
Another simple snipping activity

**Skills**
Snipping round a curved object

## What you need:

▶ Plastic or waxed paper drinking cups (coloured or patterned ones are even better)

▶ Drinking straws

▶ Dough or plasticene

## What you do:

Cutting plastic or paper cups is a good exercise for a novice cutter. The cup gives a good grip and the scissors cut down easily. Paper cups are easier to cut as they are not so sharp and brittle.

1. Look at the equipment you are going to use and explain the activity. You could have a ready-made flower to show, but this may restrict children's ability to experiment.

2. Show the children how to hold and cut the cup.

3. Let the children choose which scissors they want to use, and help them with the cutting if they need it.

4. Cut down from the edge of the cup to the bottom at regular intervals round the cup.

5. Bend the 'petals' outwards gently with fingers and thumbs.

6. Make a hole in the centre of the flower and push a straw through for a stem. Secure it with a piece of dough, plasticene or Blutack.

## And another idea

▶ Stick the flowers in a trough of sand or compost (or a block of polystyrene) to make a window box display. Add some big fringed leaves made from green card.

▶ Decorate the cups with paint before you cut them, or with shapes, beads, sequins etc. before putting the stalk through.

▶ Use muffin cups or foil jam tart trays for smaller flowers.

## Look, listen and note

▶ Watch for children who still have difficulty controlling both hands doing different things. Offer help gently.

▶ Make sure there are plenty of materials in the recycling collection for cutting, snipping and bending.

# Let it snow!

**This is a classic winter activity, but can be very satisfying at any time of year**

Skills
**Snipping folded paper**

## What you need:

▶ White paper in squares (for beginners, thinnish paper works better when folded)

▶ Scissors of all size and types

▶ Plastic plates and pencils

# What you do:

Drawing circular objects is another activity that needs co-ordination of both hands, so let the children draw their own circles using plastic plates or saucers.

1. Talk with the children about what you are going to do, showing them the equipment, and if they need it, demonstrating how to draw around a plate and cut out the circle. Help any children who are finding this bit difficult.

2. Work together to fold the circles of paper in half and then into four, so you have triangles with one curved edge.

3. Snip and cut shapes from all the edges, trying not to cut right through to the other edge!

4. Unfold your snowflakes and talk about how every one is different.

5. Once the children know how to make these patterns they can do the activity independently.

## And another idea

▶ Try different shapes – leaves folded in half, squares, triangles, flower shapes, butterflies, etc., and offer the children coloured papers – green for a spring display, or reds and oranges for autumn colours.

▶ Decorate the cut patterns with glitter, sequins or other small objects.

▶ Display the snowflakes and other patterns on windows or walls, or use them as backing for displays.

▶ Use snowflakes as stencils to make prints on paper or window glass.

## Look, listen and note

▶ Watch for children who find it difficult to cut along a line, or fold the paper. Give these children some more fine motor experiences (see page 10 for ideas).

# DIY sticker fun

**Focus**
**Make your own stickers with this easy activity**

**Skills**
**Cutting out along a guide line**

## What you need:

▶ Magazines and junk mail

▶ Scissors (a range of sorts)

▶ Water, paint brushes, pens

▶ A packet of jelly and some hot water to mix

# What you do:

This activity happens in two stages, so make sure the children understand what you are going to do. You could make some stickers beforehand, and show the children how the process works.

1. Look at the stickers you have already made, or describe carefully what you are going to do.

2. Make the jelly, letting the children watch what happens as the jelly melts.

3. Look at the magazines and junk mail and choose some pictures to make into stickers. Draw circles round the pictures so they are easier to cut out.

4. Let the children choose their own scissors and pictures to cut, and encourage them to draw their own shapes round the pictures.

5. When you have plenty of sticker pictures, use small brushes to paint the back of each picture with the warm jelly.

6. Leave the stickers to dry, and then you can lick and stick them like real stamps or stickers!

## And another idea

▶ Use wrapping paper to make character or festive stickers.

▶ Find pictures of faces or make repeated face shapes on a computer. Then use this method to make your own stamps for a role play Post Office!

▶ Use cellophane and stick the stickers to the windows. Children may need more help with cellophane as it sometimes curls when it gets wet.

## Look, listen and note

▶ Watch how children manage the different parts of this task– the drawing, cutting, pasting and sticking. You could use this activity for an informal but focussed assessment of individual children's fine motor control.

# Guess who?

**Focus**
**Making simple puppets from magazine pictures is a great way to encourage children to look carefully as they cut**

**Skills**
**Cutting along a line**

## What you need:

▶ Magazines and junk mail with lots of pictures of faces

▶ Scissors (a range of sorts)

▶ Glue and brushes or spreaders

▶ Lollipop sticks, sticky tape, card

## What you do:

This is another way of using junk mail, catalogues and magazines. It gives children practice in selecting, cutting, drawing and sticking. It's also good for discussion of characters, feelings and expressions.

1. Explain the activity, and perhaps have one or two ready made face puppets to show.

2. Give plenty of time for looking at the magazines and junk mail. Children can tear the pages they need from the magazines to make cutting easier. They may also want to draw a cutting line round the face to make it simpler.

3. Stick the faces to thin card and cut round them (using a cutting line if they want to).

4. Stick or tape a lolly stick to the back of each face picture.

5. Use the puppets to 'talk' to each other.

## And another idea

▶ Make a simple puppet theatre from a big cardboard box, or hang some fabric across a doorway.

▶ Cut the pictures from damaged or old picture books, make them into puppets, and use the puppets to re-tell the stories.

▶ Take some digital photos of the children's faces and let them make personal puppets. If you make these the size of their faces, they can pretend to be someone else!

## Look, listen and note

▶ Listen to the conversations as children select pictures. Their choices sometimes give an insight into their lives and feelings.

▶ Watch for children who are confident enough to cut without drawing their own cutting line or asking for one first.

# Wiggle, wiggle, hiss!

**Focus**
**This simple activity just uses strips of coloured paper**

**Skills**
**Cutting strips and sticking**

## What you need:

▶ Coloured construction paper

▶ A range of different types and sizes of scissors

▶ Wiggly eyes, glue, spreaders

# What you do:

Making paper chains is an easy cut and stick activity that helps scissor control and concentration. Use the chains to make snakes if it is not Christmas!

1. Cut the paper into squares or rectangles so the children can cut strips. Some children may find it easier to draw, or have you draw, guide lines so the strips end up roughly the same width.

2. Sit with the children and demonstrate how to cut the strips and join them together into circles, threading each one through the last link of the chain before sticking the ends.

3. The children should feel free to experiment with different types of scissors, and choose the colour and length of the strips they cut.

4. If making snakes from the paper chains, add a head by flattening one of the chain links after it is joined, and adding eyes and a forked tongue.

## And another idea

▶ Make colour sequences with the links, or decorate the strips with crayons, felt pens or paint before linking them.

▶ Explore other things that can be linked – make paper clip or clothes peg chains, or looped elastic bands.

## Look, listen and note

▶ Some children will really enjoy the activity and will concentrate well, making longer and longer snakes. Note those who find it difficult to concentrate, and whether this is because they find the task difficult, or generally find it difficult to sit still.

▶ For children who need more encouragement, you could use chain links of different colours to acknowledge their good behaviour and increasing concentration, such as activities completed, time spent on an activity, listening in group time etc. The child could build the chain or cut links off a ready-made chain.

# Snails on a trail!

**Focus**
**A simple cutting activity with an end product!**

**Skills**
**Cutting along a straight line**

## What you need:

▶ Paper

▶ Felt pens

▶ Glue and spreaders or brushes

▶ A range of different types and sizes of scissors

## What you do:

Cutting strips is another useful skill for practising cutting along a straight line. Some children will be able to cut strips easily, others may need cutting lines, which they draw themselves or you can draw for them.

1. Talk about what you are going to do, and demonstrate cutting strips, with and without cutting lines, and how to bend the strips round to make snails. Look at all the papers together and talk about the colours and textures. Let the children choose which colour they would like to use.

2. Let them choose whether they will cut two strips with or without cutting lines. They can then cut feelers, and put a face and patterns on one strip.

3. Help them to stick one strip into a circle with glue or sticky tape, then stick this circle onto the other strip (see picture).

4. Some children may want to make several snails!

## And another idea

▶ Make your snails into a snail mobile. Fix string onto the top of each snail's back to hang them up on coat hangers or wires.

▶ Make the snails into finger puppets by cutting a finger hole in the bottom (adult help here!) so children can use them on their index fingers as you sing 'Five Little Curly Snails'.

## Look, listen and note

▶ Watch as the children work, and note which of them have begun to cut a straight line without a cutting line, and those who can follow a cutting line.

▶ Make a note of the concentration span, and those children who particularly enjoy the cutting, while being less interested in doing anything with the strips – this is a distinct stage in scissor skill.

# Fringes

**Focus**
Another simple snipping activity

**Skills**
Fringing and sticking

## What you need:

▶ Lengths of paper in different colours

▶ A range of different types and sizes of scissors

▶ Glue (optional)

# What you do: ────────────────────

This activity puts a bit of structure into snipping, by encouraging the use of both hands and snipping along an edge. You can use any paper or thin card that is easy to cut, but make sure it is firm enough to handle in the hand that isn't holding the scissors.

1. Look at all the different papers together and talk about what you are going to do. Look at the different scissors and let the children choose which ones they would like to use. Be aware of children who may find it easier to use looped or left handed versions, and make sure they have the option of using these.

2. Sit with the children and demonstrate how to make simple cuts along the edge of the strips of paper, to make fringes.

3. The children should feel free to experiment with different types of scissors as they fringe the edges of the strips.

## And another idea ────────────────

▶ Use coloured paper to make fringed flowers. Fold some strips in half. Unfold them and fringe both sides, making sure you don't go too near the fold (a felt pen stop line may help some children).

▶ Stick the fringed strips of paper onto a paper plate to make Ollie the Octopus. Hang them in a cave with lots of cut strips of paper hanging from the ceiling.

## Look, listen and note

▶ Watch as the children work, and note any who are having difficulty. Listen to their conversations as they work, and encourage them to talk about the fringing and how they are managing the task.

▶ Make a note of any children who need help, and leave fringing activities in the art area for 'free choice' times.

# Send us a puppet!

**Focus**
A recycling activity to practice scissor skills

**Skills**
Cutting and folding

## What you need: ─────────────────────

▶ Long white A4 envelopes

▶ Other papers and card

▶ A range of types of scissors

▶ Crayons or felt pens

▶ Glue sticks

## What you do:

Used envelopes are free and are great for cutting because they give a bit more resistance than a single sheet of paper. Make sure children know not to cut up envelopes at home without permission!

1. Look at the envelopes and talk about what they are. Explain the activity. You can always demonstrate a technique or activity when you are doing it for the first time, and this helps children understand what they are doing – but don't be too perfect or you will create unachievable expectations. You might also remove your model as the children start theirs so you don't get a whole lot of identical models!

2. Stick the flap down on the envelope (or re-seal used ones with sticky tape or a glue stick.

3. Cut it in two to make two little pockets. Fold the corners in for ears.

4. Now colour the puppet and draw or stick on faces, whiskers etc.

5. Some children may want to add different eyes or ears, whiskers etc.

### And another idea

▶ Make lots of different animal puppets from envelopes and use them for a puppet show.

▶ Use frogs or other animals as puppets as you sing songs or say counting rhymes.

▶ Make people puppets and give them hats, big ears, googly eyes, fringed hair and tongues!

## Look, listen and note

▶ Note each child's level of independence and creativity in this simple activity.

▶ Encourage the children to be creative, and to stick at the task – note any who find this simple task difficult or are unable to complete it.

# Wriggly worms

**Focus**
Make a worm farm with these simple cut-and-stick worms

**Skills**
Cutting strips with or without a cutting line

## What you need:

► Paper – white and coloured
► Scissors (a range of sorts)
► Glue and spreaders or brushes
► Crayons or felt pens

## What you do:

Once children are used to marking and cutting strips, there are lots of ways to use the strips. In this activity, you could make a worm farm by covering a whole table with paper and working together as a group.

1. Explain to the children what you are going to do.

2. Let the children choose their own scissors and the paper they want to use, and help them to mark and cut strips of different widths.

3. When you have plenty of strips, cut a pointed tail and a rounded head on each strip, and decorate them with stripes and zigzags. Colour both sides of the worm, as they will be twisted in the wormery so both sides will show.

4. Draw or stick eyes on each worm.

5. Now arrange the worms on the big sheet of paper by sticking the head and tail down with blobs of glue, leaving the body in an arch above the paper. This takes a bit of practice!

6. Try arranging some worms so they twine in and out of each other.

## And another idea

▶ Use newspaper, wrapping paper, foils or holographic paper to make different worms.

▶ Sprinkle sawdust, glitter, straw or compost on the paper before sticking the worms down, to make a habitat for them.

▶ Make spiral worms by drawing a spiral and cutting along the line.

## Look, listen and note

▶ Watch for children who can use both hands confidently to do the more complex parts of this activity. Help those who need it, and give them more practice in activities where they need to use both hands.

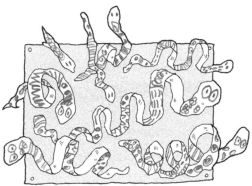

# Blowing in the wind

**Focus**
**Simple wind socks are fun when hung outside from trees, bushes or a fence**

**Skills**
**Cutting with or without lines, sticking, using a hole punch**

## What you need:

▶ A piece of thin white card about 15cm x 45cm for each child

▶ Scissors (a range of sorts)

▶ Glue and brushes or spreaders

▶ Crêpe paper, stapler, hole punch

▶ Ribbon, paint or felt pens

# What you do:

Cutting and sticking to make something that works is a great motivator, and boys will love these wind socks that they can run about with outdoors.

1. Explain the activity, by having a ready made wind sock for the children to look at. If possible, take it outside so they can see how it works.

2. Let the children divide their piece of card into sections using a felt pen or crayon, and make a different design or colour in each section – stripes, circles, wavy lines, dots, stars, etc.

3. Show the children how to cut slices off a roll of crêpe paper to make streamers. The slices will make long streamers that may need to be cut into sections. Stick some of these streamers (or lengths of ribbon) along the back of the short edge of the card.

4. Help the children to roll the card into a tube, and staple it together, so the streamers are at the end of the tube.

5. Punch two holes at the other end of the tube, and thread a ribbon through for a 'handle'. Hang your wind socks up outside, or run with them.

## And another idea

▶ Use snack tubes or cereal boxes for wind sock bodies.

▶ Try different materials for streamers – ribbon, wool, tinsel, or strips from plastic bags.

▶ Make windmills, wind vanes, parachutes or sailing boats.

## Look, listen and note

▶ Look at the way different children decorate their wind socks. Some will take care and time, others may only be interested in going outside and trying them!

▶ Offer plenty of recycled materials for cutting, snipping and experimenting.

# Rock-a-bye birdie

**Focus**
**A simple rocking toy that children can make by themselves**

**Skills**
**Cutting along a curved line**

## What you need:

▶ Construction paper or thin card

▶ A range of types of scissors

▶ Plastic plates

▶ Decorations such as feathers, sequins and shiny paper

▶ Glue

## What you do: ────────────

This is an independent activity which children can manage themselves once they have basic scissor skills. Younger or less experienced children may need some help.

1. Use the plastic plates to draw circles.
2. Fold each circle in half – this is the body of your 'bird'!
3. Cut or colour simple wing shapes on the bird's sides.
4. Make a beak from paper, and decorate the bird with sequins and other materials. Don't forget to decorate both sides.
5. Cut a circle of paper or thin card for the birds head, and attach it to the body using a peg.
6. Give the bird an eye on each side of its head, and a fringed paper or feather tail attached with another peg.
7. Open the bird gently and it will stand up. Push it gently and it will rock to and fro.

## And another idea ────────────

▶ Experiment with smaller or larger circles to make bird families.
▶ Use the birds in collage or other displays, linked with stories about birds. Make some nests from twigs or hay, and some eggs from playdough.
▶ Make other standing animals – a square for an elephant, a triangle for a cat.

## Look, listen and note

▶ Note the children who can draw round the plate with ease, and help those who can't.

▶ Listen for ideas and extensions to conversations as the children experiment with materials and equipment.

▶ Use language such as 'bigger' and 'smaller', 'longer' and 'shorter' to describe objects and resources.

# A very handy tree!

**Focus**
This activity gives more practice at using both hands in co-ordination

**Skills**
Drawing around hands and cutting out

## What you need:

▶ Coloured paper

▶ Pencils, drinking straws, twigs, clay or dough

▶ A range of different types and sizes of scissors

## What you do:

Drawing around your own hand takes some practice and skill. Some children will need help from an adult, or to work in pairs.

1. Explain what you are going to do and show them how to draw around their own hand, or their friend's hand. Younger or less experienced cutters may like to keep their fingers together as they draw round the hand. Older, more experienced cutters may like to spread their fingers out. You may like to remind them that the outlines of spread fingers are more difficult to cut out.

2. Let them do several hand outlines and then cut them out.

3. Make a tree by tying some twigs together and standing them in a big lump of clay or dough (or a plant pot filled with sand).

4. Stick, hang, or tie the hands onto the tree to make leaves.

## And another idea

▶ Use hand shapes to make a wreath (cut a big circle and stick the hands in an overlapping pattern around the edge).

▶ Make flowers by sticking the hands onto a circle of card (fingers facing out).

▶ Make hand 'puppets' by drawing faces on the palms and sticking wool hair on the fingers. Then stick them onto a lolly stick or straw.

▶ Make a paper peacock and use the hand shapes as feathers

## Look, listen and note

▶ Watch as the children work, and note any who become easily frustrated by the task; these children may need more opportunities to practice in short tasks to build their confidence and concentration.

▶ Watch how children co-operate on a shared task, helping each other and taking turns.

# Make a shape

**Focus**
**Drawing and cutting shapes**

**Skills**
**Cutting along straight and curved lines**

## What you need:

▶ Thin card

▶ A range of types of scissors

▶ Glue, felt pens, crayons

▶ Plates, saucers, bricks and other shapes to draw around

# What you do:

You may want to prepare a few shapes before you start so you can show the children what they could make with them, but making the shapes is an important part of the activity so don't do it all for them.

1. Help the children to draw around the objects onto the thin card to make squares, rectangles and circles of different sizes. They can cut the shapes out and colour them with crayons or felt pens.

2. Try cutting some of the shapes in half to make semi-circles and triangles.

3. Now use your shapes to make faces of people or animals, starting with a big circle, and adding other shapes for eyes, ears, a mouth, etc. Make more shapes if they need them.

4. When the children are happy with their cardboard faces, stick the features down.

## And another idea

▶ Use the shapes for a fishing game by adding paper clips and fishing with a magnet on a string.

▶ Go on a shape template hunt to see how many objects you can find to make different shape templates.

▶ Laminate some of the shapes so they last longer, and make some shape matching games.

▶ Make tactile shapes from sandpaper, fur fabric, plastic, cork sheet, etc.

## Look, listen and note

▶ Note the children who use their imagination in making the faces and other shape pictures. Some children will be very quick to recognise shapes in the environment.

▶ Use the activity as a gentle way to find out whether individual children can recognise and name simple shapes.

43

# Let's go fly a kite!

**Focus**
**Paper plate kites are easy to make and fly well in any weather**

**Skills**
**Cutting strips, ribbons and string; using a hole punch**

## What you need:

▶ Large white paper plates

▶ Scissors (a range of sorts)

▶ Felt pens, ribbon, wool, crêpe paper, string

▶ Hole punch, stapler

## What you do:

This is a good impromptu activity for a windy day, and can be done without too much adult help. Just show the children what to do, make sure they have all the resources they need, and then sit and watch what happens. It's a good activity for structured observation of the skills of a couple of individual children.

1. Collect the materials, sit with the children and talk about what you are going to do. You could make a sample as the children watch, talking the activity through then leaving them to make their own kites, asking for help from other children or you if they need it.

2. Each child needs a paper plate. The following instructions are just a guide.

3. Punch four holes round the sides of the plate for the strings.

4. Draw shapes, patterns or faces on the paper plate.

5. Cut some streamers from ribbon, crêpe paper or wool, and make more holes to tie them on the plate.

6. Measure and cut four equal pieces of string and tie one through each of the four holes. Tie the other ends together at the front of the plate (so you can see the pattern as it flies) and add another piece to hold on to.

7. Now go outside and fly your kites.

## And another idea

▶ Make kites from other shapes of card – squares, triangles, diamonds – which work best?

▶ Make plastic bag kites from carrier bags, by cutting the end off the bag and tying the handles together. Cut streamers from strips of other bags, and stick them on with sticky tape.

▶ Sing windy or flying songs as you work and as you fly your kites outside.

## Look, listen and note

▶ As suggested, use this activity as a chance to observe children working independently. See how well they cope, how their skills are developing, and how they help each other.

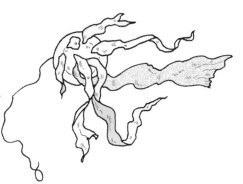

# Colourful caterpillars

**Focus**
**Lots of practice at drawing around and cutting curved lines**

**Skills**
**Cutting curved and straight lines, Velcro, paper fasteners**

## What you need:

▶ Thin card – white or coloured

▶ Round objects to draw around

▶ Scissors (a range of sorts)

▶ Glue and brushes or spreaders

▶ Small Velcro dots or paper fasteners

▶ Sequins, beads, pens, glitter

# What you do:

This activity gives children plenty of practice in drawing around circular objects and cutting along curved lines. Choose template objects that suit the ability level of the group, and offer a selection – the caterpillars can be any size!

1. Explain the activity, and show the children how to select and draw around the templates and cut them out.

2. Let the children choose, draw around and cut out some circles.

3. Talk about how they can decorate the circles with pens and other items. Give plenty of time for this part of the activity.

4. Encourage the children to make a head from one of the circles and draw a face. Add some feelers made from paper or wool.

5. Use the Velcro dots to join the circles together. Show the children what to do, but then let them decide where to put their own dots.

6. The circles should overlap each other as the caterpillar grows.

## And another idea

▶ Let the children experiment with taking the caterpillars apart and sticking them back together. They could make a big caterpillar by joining their circles and those of their friends.

▶ Punch holes in the circles and use treasury tags to join them. Or stick magnetic tape on the back and use a metal tray to make the caterpillar.

▶ Make colour sequence caterpillars or use big/small/big/small circles.

▶ Use the caterpillars to play 'One More' and 'One Less' games.

## Look, listen and note

▶ Encourage the children to use their caterpillars in informal activities. Watch what they do and note any unusual ideas they have. Offer more practice by leaving the materials out during child-initiated sessions, when children can revisit and practice skills.

# Shape transformers

**Focus**
You need some popper fasteners for this activity - see page 70 for suppliers

**Skills**
Cutting lines, popper fasteners, hole punch

## What you need:

▶ Coloured and white card

▶ Shapes to draw around bricks for rectangles, plates for circles, etc.

▶ Different types of scissors

▶ Hole punch, popper fasteners

I will need

## What you do:

This activity gives children practice with making shapes and then joining them together to make sequences, pictures and patterns. Popper fasteners are one easy way to join card shapes, but you could use paper fasteners. Laminating the shapes, covering them with sticky backed plastic or painting them with white glue will protect them and make them last much longer.

1. Work with the children to draw around shapes on the card and cut them out. You could paint them, or make patterns on them to make them more fun to use. Turning simple shapes into other well-known objects or things by making faces, tyres, buttons, eyes, windows, numbers, letters etc. will encourage children to invent and think creatively.

2. Protect the shapes with plastic, white glue or lamination if you like.

3. Now help the children to put the popper fasteners on the shapes - each shape will need at least two poppers in different places, so the combinations are more complex.

4. Now see how many combinations the children can make by popping the shapes together.

## And another idea

▶ Make lots of squares, circles, triangles and rectangles, and use them to make sequences and patterns.

▶ Challenge the children to make a car, a clown, a house, a truck, a person.

▶ Make some more shapes from thick felt or tough fabrics such as denim.

▶ Make a huge design with all the shapes.

## Look, listen and note

▶ Look for children who are beginning to be confident when drawing round objects, cutting along curved and straight lines, and turning corners.

▶ Note the unusual ideas children have when their imagination or humour is triggered. Photograph some of these for an ideas book or display.

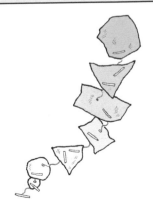

# Dancing puppets

**Focus**
Make some of these simple 'dancing' puppets which are easy for young children to use

**Skills**
Cutting, fringing, sticking

## What you need:

▶ White card

▶ A range of different types and sizes of scissors

▶ Pencils, pens, decorations such as wool and sticky paper

# What you do:

Children can make their puppets dance by putting their fingers through the holes in the puppet. Making and operating the puppets is good fine motor practice.

1. Talk with the children about the puppets you are going to make. You could look at the 'Mr Men' books, as they have simple shape characters.

2. Use templates such as bricks or plastic beakers to draw shapes on card – circles, ovals, triangles, squares, rectangles.

3. Let the children choose the shapes, draw and cut them out.

4. Make the two circular holes at the bottom of the puppet for fingers to go through (this is an adult bit, and needs pointed scissors, which children will probably find too difficult).

5. Use felt pens and other small items to decorate the puppets.

6. The puppets are ready to dance!

## And another idea

▶ Make character puppets for stories – start with some 'Mr Men' characters.

▶ Cover a table with a sheet of paper, tape it down and help the children to draw a plan or map on the paper. Take the puppets for a walk or tell a story.

## Look, listen and note

▶ Watch how the children manage the task and make the puppet dance, which is another fine motor skill. Help children who need it by demonstrating, or using a puppet on your own hand to dance or tell a story together.

▶ Listen to their conversations as they work and as they make the puppets dance, walk or simply greet each other!

# Cool cones!

**Focus**
**Making cones is another skill that needs both hands**

**Skills**
**Cutting, folding, hole punch, cone making**

## What you need:

▶ Brown, yellow or orange construction paper

▶ Different types of scissors

▶ Sticky tape, cotton wool

▶ Sequins, glitter or the 'holes' from hole punches for 'sprinkles'

52

# What you do:

Making coloured dots from paper with a hole punch is an activity some children love – and it strengthens hand muscles! Using both hands to make a cone from a triangle is a skill that uses fingers, hands and wrists. It may take some practice and children may need your help at this stage, but support them in being as independent as possible.

1. Explain and demonstrate what you are going to do – you could suggest making an ice-cream stall or a van, then show the children how to make the 'ice cream cones'.

2. Cut some squares from the paper. Fold each square in half, corner to corner, to make a triangle. Unfold again and cut along the fold to make two triangles.

3. Curl each triangle around to make a cone, and secure it with a piece of tape. Most children will need help with this bit.

4. Fill the top of the cone with some cotton wool, and decorate with 'sprinkles' of your choice.

## And another idea

▶ Make a role play ice-cream parlour or ice-cream van.

▶ Create larger, flatter cones to make hats, then thread a piece of ribbon, wool or thin elastic through to hold the hat on.

▶ Make bigger cones for megaphones and experiment with these outside.

## Look, listen and note

▶ Watch how the children work, using hands, wrist, fingers, and how they use both hands together.

▶ Continue to note which scissors they prefer and how their scissor skills are developing.

▶ Listen to conversations and join these to model new vocabulary.

# My special headband

**Focus**
Another simple snipping activity

**Skills**
Cutting on a line, stapling, sticking, snipping

## What you need:

▶ Thin card

▶ A range of scissors

▶ Pens and other materials to decorate

▶ Glue, a stapler

## What you do:

Headbands are great for all sorts of role play, and children can, and should, learn how to make them for themselves. Then they can incorporate them in their own free play. Show them how to make crowns, simple character bands, animals and other creatures, then just provide the resources.

1. Draw cutting lines 10 – 12cm apart on card. Let the children cut along the lines to make the basic bands.

2. Each child can make one or more bands by decorating the strips before joining them to fit their head. Try:

   ▶ sticking on fur fabric, ribbon, jewels or sequins;

   ▶ drawing patterns or making designs for characters;

   ▶ cutting points or other shapes along the strip.

3. Use a stapler or tape to join the band to fit.

4. Add ears, feelers, googly eyes on stalks, ribbons, 'hair', ears or anything else they fancy.

## And another idea

▶ Make themed sets of headbands – jungle animals, pets, superheroes, kings and queens, space creatures etc., and keep in themed boxes or bags for free play or group storytelling.

▶ Make some seasonal or special occasion bands and have a parade, picnic, celebration or party.

## Look, listen and note

▶ Watch for creativity and imagination in using the resources you have offered. Make sure children have plenty of inspiration and try not to influence the sort of design ideas they may have.

▶ Keep noting successes and difficulties in fine motor control and concentration. Provide additional opportunities to practice fine motor skills – they are especially helpful to many boys.

# Wheels, wheels, wheels

**Focus**
Vehicle pictures from all sorts of shapes

**Skills**
Cutting along a fold, along straight and curved lines

## What you need:

▶ Construction paper, all colours

▶ Scissors (a range of sorts)

▶ Glue and spreaders or brushes

▶ Foil, patterned papers and other objects for decoration

▶ A roll of wallpaper, coloured frieze paper or lining paper

I will need

# What you do:

Use squares and rectangles, with some circles for wheels, in this vehicle construction activity.

1. Talk with the children about the activity, and explain that you need to make lots of squares, rectangles and circles to make one big picture of all sorts of vehicles – cars, lorries, buses, fire-engines and motor bikes.

2. Look at the long roll of paper and decide together if you will make a street, a car park, a motorway or any other picture. You could paint a road, shops, fields, houses or other background if you like.

3. Cut some pieces of coloured construction paper and help the children to make squares, rectangles and circles. Cut some smaller squares and circles from foil or shiny paper to make windows and wheel hubs.

4. Work with the children to make vehicles from the shapes, making them first on a table, then when they are happy with the design, sticking them on the background.

## And another idea

▶ Cut patterned and textured paper into shapes to make houses, trees and people for your frieze.

▶ Add more shapes, such as semi-circles, triangles or stars to add detail to your pictures.

▶ Make a bus from rectangles and circles for wheels, and draw faces on small circles for the driver and passengers.

## Look, listen and note

▶ Observe this activity carefully, to see how children cope with a bigger project that involves thinking and planning ahead, working together and negotiating the plans.

▶ Give plenty of time for talk, and listen carefully to what children say about what they are doing.

# Clowning around

**Focus**
These clowns make an eye-catching display, frieze or colourful masks for songs

**Skills**
Cutting shapes, fringing, sticking

## What you need:

▶ Large paper plates

▶ Scissors (a range of sorts)

▶ Pens, paint, sticky paper

▶ Glue and brushes or spreaders

▶ Lolly sticks or chopsticks, tape

I will need

# What you do:

This activity combines cutting straight and curved lines, cone making, fringing, curling, using templates to draw round, sticking and joining.

1. Explain the activity and talk about what clowns look like – red noses, white faces, big smiles, etc. You could look at some pictures of clowns in stories or on the internet.

2. Remind the children of the different techniques they could use, and demonstrate curling or fringing paper or cutting lengths of wool for hair, marking cutting lines, using a triangle or other shapes to make a cone for a hat, or two triangles to make a bow tie.

3. Look at the resources together, then give the children as much freedom as possible to construct their clown face, fetching objects to draw round and using techniques and skills to make their own unique version.

4. Make the finished clown faces into masks by punching a hole in each side for a string, or turn them into puppets by sticking a short stick or chopstick on the back.

## And another idea

▶ Children could make their own bow ties from fabric or crêpe paper and wear a clown mask above it.

▶ Make some paper flowers and use them for tricks.

▶ Peg the clown masks on a washing line to make a great decoration, then use them for counting games.

## Look, listen and note

▶ Use the activity as a recap of skills already demonstrated and see how many of the children can remember and use the simpler skills they learned earlier.

▶ Make a note of how many different skills each child remembers and uses in this activity.

# There's a mouse in my house!

**Focus**
Another simple cone-making activity

**Skills**
Cutting, making small cones, sticking

## What you need:

▶ Coloured paper

▶ Wool for tails

▶ Paint or felt pens, tape, glue

▶ A range of different types and sizes of scissors

I will need

# What you do:

Children may still need a bit of help making cones, but they can complete the rest of the activity themselves.

1. Talk about the mice you are going to make and have an example for the children to look at before you start.

2. Use a saucer or the top of a plastic beaker as a template to draw a circle on a piece of paper. Cut the circle out.

3. Fold the circle in half, unfold it and cut along the fold to make two circles. Make one of the semi-circles into a cone for the mouse body and stick it with tape or glue.

4. Draw some small ovals on the other semi-circle, cut them out and stick them near the top of the cone for ears.

5. Draw a little nose, some black eyes and whiskers with felt pen.

6. Cut a length of wool for a tail and stick the end inside the cone.

7. Put the puppet on your finger to make it move.

## And another idea

▶ Use the mice for songs and counting rhymes such as:

Five little mice came out to play,
Gathering crumbs along the way,
Out came pussycat sleek and fat,
Four little mice go scampering back.
(repeat with 4, 3, 2, 1, 0)

## Look, listen and note

▶ Note how the children's skills and hand control are developing.

▶ Plan more activities to support children who need more practice in using their hands and fingers to make simple pictures, toys and objects.

▶ Continue to offer children plenty of free access to tools and resources for cutting, snipping and constructing with card and paper to make props for role play and their own creations.

# Through the windows

**Focus**
**This activity is suitable for children who have more developed fine motor control**

**Skills**
**More complex cutting, folding, sticking**

## What you need:

▶ Black paper

▶ Coloured plastic sweet wrappers, or coloured cellophane

▶ A range of different types and sizes of scissors

# What you do:

This activity builds on the snowflake activity earlier in this book by adding cellophane colours to the gaps, so they resemble stained glass.

1. Talk with the children about what you are going to do. Show them some pictures of stained glass in books or on the internet. Remind them of the way to make snowflake patterns from circles of paper.

2. Look at the coloured cellophane or sweet wrappers; hold them up to the light and discuss the colours.

3. Cut some squares and circles together, using cutting lines and circle templates.

4. Fold the shapes in half, then in quarters. Cut some shapes out from the edges of the folded shape.

5. Unfold the shape and cut some coloured cellophane pieces to to cover the holes. Stick these in place with small dabs of glue or a glue stick.

6. Stick the finished creations on a window to get the full effect.

## And another idea

▶ Make easier stained glass by cutting or tearing coloured tissue into pieces (the pieces can be any shape). Paste the shapes with diluted white glue to a sheet of plastic such as an opened-up black bin bag. Make sure you stick the pieces down well and brush some of the glue over the top. Leave to dry and then peel the sheet off the plastic and cut it into shapes for decorating windows, cards and gift tags.

## Look, listen and note

▶ Make a simple check-sheet of scissor skills (using the progression on page 10) and use this to check where children are, and who needs more practice in individual skills.

# Chinese lanterns

**Focus**
Folding and cutting on cutting lines

**Skills**
Folding, cutting even strips, stopping before a fold

## What you need:

▶ Coloured paper

▶ A range of different types and sizes of scissors

▶ Glue stick

# What you do:

This activity is a simple application of drawing and cutting along straight lines. Once they have been shown how, children can make more lanterns independently.

1. Prepare some rectangles of paper about 30m x 20cm.

2. Show the children how to fold the rectangles in half with the long edges together.

3. Cut a narrow strip about 2cm wide from the end of the folded sheet (this is for the handle).

4. Now mark cutting lines at equal distances along the rest of the fold, stopping short of the cut edge. Cut along each line.

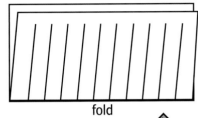

fold

5. Unfold the lantern and use the glue stick to join the short edges into a cylinder. Attach the handle to the top of the lantern.

## And another idea

▶ Hang the lanterns on a line across a window as a decoration.

▶ Make lanterns big enough to go over an empty jam jar and carefully light a tea light inside. Lighted lanterns should always be placed where children cannot reach them.

▶ Make lanterns from wallpaper, wrapping paper or foil to make decorations for different festivals. Attach these to the end of canes and have a parade.

## Look, listen and note

▶ Some children may be able to make the cuts without drawing cutting lines. Observe and note these developing skills and confidence.

▶ Make sure children always have a choice of types and sizes of scissors to choose from, and be aware that hand dominance develops slowly and some children my be ambidextrous for some time.

# A 'handy' lamb

**Focus**
**A more complex use for simple hand prints**

**Skills**
**Cutting out along a line, sticking**

## What you need:

▶ Coloured paper or thin card (pastel colours work best)

▶ A variety of scissors

▶ Black and white paint and brushes

▶ Cotton wool, googly eyes

▶ Glue sticks

I will need

# What you do:

Making hand prints is another way of encouraging personalised cutting. Remember, some children still find cutting out difficult, so encourage these children to keep their fingers closed as they make the prints. This makes the cutting out easier.

1. Look at the equipment you are going to use and explain the activity, showing the children your example if you feel they need it. Having a ready made 'lamb' to show helps, as the concept is a bit difficult to visualise.

2. Help the children to paint their hand with black paint and make a print on pale-coloured card or paper.

3. When this is dry, let the children choose some scissors to cut it out.

4. Turn the hand print so the fingers point down to make the legs, and the thumb will becomes the head end. Stick cotton wool on the palm area for the body.

5. Stick a wiggly eye on the thumb head. Display your 'handy lambs' as a flock on a field of green paper.

## And another idea

▶ Use the same method to make other animals or figures – a ghost, a brown horse, a jellyfish, etc.

▶ Use hand and footprints to make or composite pictures, such as a hand sunflower, a tree with footprint leaves, or a Christmas wreath.

▶ Print on sandpaper or corrugated card.

## Look, listen and note

▶ If cutting out the fingers is to difficult for some children, draw a cutting line to help them.

▶ Watch for children who really don't like paint on their skin. They could wear a plastic glove to do the activity. Gloves are also useful for children who have eczema or other allergic reactions.

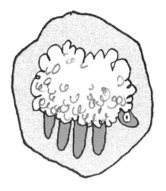

# Spiral snakes

**Focus**
**Following a spiral line – a more difficult task!**

**Skills**
**Cutting along a spiral line, hole punch**

## What you need:

▶ Paper plates

▶ Scissors (a range of sorts)

▶ Paint, pens

▶ Materials to decorate the plate

▶ String or wool to hang the snakes up

# What you do:

If you use paint, this activity will happen in two stages, so make sure the children understand what you are going to do. You could make a snake of your own first, and show the children how the process works.

1. Discuss the resources and the process of making the snake – show your snake on the table before pulling it up on the string, so they can see how the paper plate turns into the snake.
2. Paint the plate on both sides and leave to dry.
3. Now draw a spiral from the centre of the plate to the edge – some children will be able to do this themselves. Help any who need it, but try to let them do as much as possible, even if it is a bit wobbly.
4. Now let them choose scissors to cut along the spiral line.
5. Draw some eyes on the head end, and stick on a forked red tongue.
6. Make a hole near the head and thread some string through to hang it up.
7. Decorate the snakes by gently letting them down onto a flat surface while you colour them or stick things on.

## And another idea

▶ Hang your snakes above a table display of sand, stones and plants in a builder's tray. Hang some crêpe paper or fabric leaves and creepers up with them.

▶ Use spirals to make Christmas or other festival decorations.

▶ Use plastic plates for some outdoor spirals that spin in the wind.

## Look, listen and note

▶ Some children may find cutting a paper plate difficult, because their hand muscles are not strong enough. These children could work with flat card or strong paper. Don't do the cutting for them or their muscles and control will never develop!

# Resources and suppliers

## Websites for more craft activity ideas
www.enchantedlearning.com
www.preschoolexpress.com
www.perpetualpreschool.com
www.preschooleducation.com

## Books
Learn to Cut, by Robin R. Wolfe
Cutting Skills, by Mark & Katy Hill
Developing Basic Scissor Skills, by Sue Mahoney and Alison Markwell
Scissor Skills, by Dorothy Penso

# Suppliers

Peta (UK) Ltd: www.peta-uk.com
Tel: +44(0)1376 573476 E-mail: info@peta-uk.com
Peta have a wide range of specialist scissors for children and adults, including self opening versions, long loop, scissors on stands and dual control scissors.

Berol: www.berol.co.uk
Stockists of Milly Scissors, in left and right handed versions, which have a finger grip area to ensure correct finger position. Berol also have many other sorts of scissors in right and left handed versions, including zigzag and other decorative blades. They also stock scissor blocks for storing and checking scissors.

Anything Left-Handed: www.anythingleft-handed.co.uk
Suppliers of left-handed scissors for children and adults, and a range of other items for left-handers, including pencil sharpeners.

http://video.about.com/babyparenting/Using-Scissors.htm
Features a very good video and transcript for parents on teaching scissor skills and safety, which is also useful for students and others new to scissor teaching.

Google 'magnetic tape' to find suppliers and dispensers, or you could ask at a DIY store or your school/early years science supply catalogue. Alternatively, order rolls of magnetic tape from www.commotiongroup.co.uk

Get pop fasteners from market stalls, haberdashers, craft shops or sewing stores.

Velcro Dots are also available in DIY stores or sewing shops, but if you want a bigger quantity, get them on a roll from websites such as www.FASTENation.com

# The Little Books Club

There is always something in Little Books to help and inspire you. Packed full of lovely ideas, Little Books meet the need for exciting and practical activities that are fun to do, address the Early Learning Goals and can be followed in most settings. Everyone is a winner!

We publish 5 new Little Books a year. Little Books Club members receive each of these 5 books as soon as they are published for a reduced price. The subscription cost is £29.99 – a one off payment that buys the 5 new books for £4.99 instead of £8.99 each.

In addition to this, Little Books Club Members receive:
· Free postage and packing on anything ordered from the Featherstone catalogue
· A 15% discount voucher upon joining which can be used to buy any number of books from the Featherstone catalogue
· Members price of £4.99 on any additional Little Book purchased
· A regular, free newsletter dealing with club news, special offers and aspects of Early Years curriculum and practice
· All new Little Books on approval - return in good condition within 30 days and we'll refund the cost to your club account

Call 020 7458 0200 or email: littlebooks@bloomsbury.com for an enrolment pack. Or download an application form from our website:

## www.bloomsbury.com

# The **Little Books** series consists of:

50
All through the year
Bags, Boxes & Trays
Big Projects
Bricks & Boxes
Celebrations
Christmas
Circle Time
Clay and Malleable
Materials
Clothes and Fabric
Colour, Shape & Number
Cooking from Stories
Cooking Together
Counting
Dance
Dance Music CD
Dens
Discovery Bottles
Dough
Drama from Stories
Explorations
Fine Motor Skills
Free and Found
Fun on a Shoestring
Games with Sounds
Gross Motor Skills
Growing Things
ICT
Investigations
Junk Music

Kitchen Stuff
Language Fun
Light and Shadow
Listening
Living Things
Look and Listen
Making Books and Cards
Making Poetry
Maps and Plans
Mark Making
Maths Activities
Maths from Stories
Maths Outdoors
Maths Problem Solving
Maths Songs & Games
Messy Play
Minibeast Hotels
Multi-sensory Stories
Music
Nursery Rhymes
Opposites
Outdoor Play
Outside in All Weathers
Painting
Parachute Play
Persona Dolls
Phonics
Playground Games
Prop Boxes for Role Play
Props for Writing
Puppet Making

Puppets in Stories
Resistant Materials
Rhythm and Raps
Role Play
Role Play Windows
Sand and Water
Science through Art
Scissor Skills
Seasons
Sequencing Skills
Sewing and Weaving
Small World Play
Sound Ideas
Special Days
Stories from around the
world
Story bags
Storyboards
Storybuilding
Storytelling
Time and Money
Time and Place
Topsy Turvy
Traditional Tales
Treasure Baskets
Treasure Boxes
Tuff Spot Activities
Washing lines
Woodwork
Writing

## All available from
# www.bloomsbury.com